Money Around the World

What Is Money?

Rebecca Rissman

KU-153-091

Heinemann
LIBRARY

www.heinemann.co.uk/library
Visit our website to find out more information about Heinemann Library books.

To order:
☎ Phone 44 (0) 1865 888066
▤ Send a fax to 44 (0) 1865 314091
💻 Visit the Heinemann Bookshop at www.heinemann.co.uk/library to browse our catalogue and order online.

ABERDEENSHIRE LIBRARY AND INFORMATION SERVICES

	2623581
HJ	680131
J332.4	£9.50
JU	JNF

First published in Great Britain by Heinemann Library, Halley Court, Jordan Hill, Oxford OX2 8EJ, part of Harcourt Education. Heinemann is a registered trademark of Harcourt Education Ltd.

© Harcourt Education Ltd 2008
The moral right of the proprietor has been asserted.

All rights reserved. No part of this publication may be reproduced, stored in a retrieval system, or transmitted in any form or by any means, electronic, mechanical, photocopying, recording, or otherwise, without either the prior written permission of the publishers or a licence permitting restricted copying in the United Kingdom issued by the Copyright Licensing Agency Ltd, 90 Tottenham Court Road, London W1T 4LP (www.cla.co.uk).

Editorial: Diyan Leake
Design: Joanna Hinton-Malivoire and Steve Mead
Picture research: Tracy Cummins and Heather Mauldin
Production: Duncan Gilbert

Origination: Chroma Graphics (Overseas) Pte Ltd
Printed and bound in China by South China Printing Company Ltd

ISBN 978 0 431 02527 8
12 11 10 09 08
10 9 8 7 6 5 4 3 2 1

British Library Cataloguing in Publication Data
Rissman, Rebecca
 What is money? - (Money around the world)
 1. Money - Juvenile literature
 I. Title
 332.4

Acknowledgments
The author and publisher are grateful to the following for permission to reproduce copyright material: © Getty Images pp. **4**, **5**, **6** (AFP/Atta Kenare), **8** (Oliver Benn), **9** (AFP/Kazuhiro Nogi), **10** (Darren Robb), **13** (Olaf Tiedje), **14** (Gary John Norman), **15** (Andrew Hetherington), **16** (Keith Brofsky), **17** (Stephen Derr), **18** (AFP/Kim Jae-Hwan), **19** (Altrendo Images), **20** (Lorne Resnick), **21** (Absodels), **23a** (Chien-min Chung), **23b** (Cosmo Condina), **back cover** (Gary John Norman); © istockphoto pp. **11** (Ilya Genkin, **12** (Sean Lock); © Masterfile p. **22** (Royalty Free); © The World Bank p. **7** (Curt Carnemark).

Cover photograph reproduced with permission of © istockphoto (Ilya Genkin).

Every effort has been made to contact copyright holders of any material reproduced in this book. Any omissions will be rectified in subsequent printings if notice is given to the publisher.

Contents

What is money?

People use money.

People use money to pay for things.

taxi driver

When people work, they are paid money.

6

When people buy things, they
spend money.

People use money to get things
they want.

People use money to get things
they need.

Types of money

Coins are money.

Bank notes are money.

Cheques are a type of money.

Debit cards and credit cards are a type of money.

Using money

People use coins to buy things.

People use bank notes to buy things.

People use cheques to buy things.

People use debit cards or credit cards to buy things.

Some things cost a little money.

Some things cost a lot of money.

Money around the world

All around the world, people use money.

What do you spend your money on?

Different kinds of money

Money looks different around the world.

Picture glossary

 **money** bank notes, coins, cheques, debit cards, or credit cards, which are used to pay for work or for things

 **pay** give money to get something back

Index

Notes for parents and teachers

Before reading

Talk to the children about money. Show them some coins and notes and ask them how people get money and what they do with their money.

After reading

• Give the children a selection of different coins and show them how to do a coin rubbing. Place a coin under a piece of paper. Using a soft pencil, scribble over the paper to see the imprint of the coin appear. Make a pattern of different coin rubbings.

• Start a collection of different money from around the world. Compare the coins from different countries. Use a globe to show where the currency comes from.

• Sing the song: "I've got sixpence, Jolly, jolly sixpence".